Bacon

Francis Bacon

Ediciones Polígrafa

Francis Bacon in his studio, where he often used the walls and door as a palette

4

The Realism of Francis Bacon

It is not unusual to hear the paintings of Francis Bacon described as Expressionist. Yet that label greatly annoyed the British painter, displeasing him even more than other, quite unflattering characterizations of his work. Most artists associated with Expressionism sought to project their emotions onto the world, deforming or distorting appearances toward that expressive end. Such art can, therefore, be considered idealist; exaggerated facial traits, for example, can flaunt the subject's distance from an imagined ideal.

Bacon's works have in common with some modes of Expressionism in modern art the violence of the pictorial gesture and the immediate effect of shock, but they could be considered Expressionist only in a very general sense. The artist himself summed up his work as an attempt to capture, through the painted image of the body, the sensations that its physical reality stirred within him. For Bacon, abstract art held little appeal; the human figure was the fundamental, and almost the only, subject. The figure is subjected to distortion in Bacon's work for reasons different from those of the Expressionists: what he seeks is to mock the routine, superficial way we generally look at ourselves and the world. He seeks to overturn conventions associated with everyday perception in order to bring the viewer closer to the raw fact of corporeal life. The objective is to upset the stability of the ordinary point of view, breaking down the protective barriers separating us from the immediacy of experience.

The Theater of the Body

Perhaps the term that best describes Bacon's work is "realism," a classification that is often employed too loosely but which here is meant in a special sense. In this case, realism does not mean direct, straightforward representation—something Bacon dismissed as mere "illustration," and from which he felt as far removed as from abstract painting. Instead it means a fidelity to the vital experience of living inside the body, which for him is a fundamental theme of art. Like the realists of the nineteenth century, Bacon scrupulously recorded the mobile, shifting reality of the human form with the means that painting placed at his disposal. The difference is that by Bacon's time, a century later, the arsenal of resources for painting is much greater; naturalistic, imitative criteria are no longer sufficient. Bacon's realism is, therefore, radically modern, and his point of departure, as he freely admitted, was Pablo Picasso's work from the late 1920s, which is sometimes considered Surrealist, though of an unusually tough-minded kind.

George Dyer, the most frequent model in Bacon's paintings until 1971, the year of Dyer's death.

The painter Lucian Freud, Bacon's friend and model, with whose works he has a certain affinity.

Isabel Rawsthorne, another frequent subject in Bacon's canvases, particularly in the 1960s.

Velázquez's Pope Innocent X, *1650, a famous painting that obsessed Bacon in the 1950s.*

Photo-booth snapshots of Francis Bacon, like those used often for his self-portraits.

Photograph of wrestlers by Eadweard Muybridge that gave rise to several of Bacon's paintings.

The drama in Bacon's painting arises from the fact that, inevitably, the viewer cannot help but identify to some extent with what a picture shows. The distortion of the body's ordinary appearance in a painting can make us cringe with a new and discomforting sense of how human flesh and bone are constituted. With Bacon, the figure often appears at the edge of dissolution, just prior to becoming unrecognizable. The painter concentrates all the violence of the brushstroke in the human form, using the agitated pictorial material to embody the convulsions of the flesh. To achieve this effect, Bacon at times hurls handfuls of paint against the canvas, forming it subsequently with his hands, the paintbrush, or other direct means. In these ways he affirms his presence in all its "brutality of fact."

An Enclosed Space

In contrast, the space surrounding the figures is rigorously orthodox: the spatial boxes around the figures or the curves bending behind them are extensions of the viewer's own space. Critics have often attempted to see these boxes as an existentialist metaphor of anonymous, desolate places, like sordid rooms in cheap hotels, or prison cells; however, Bacon's painting resists any symbolic interpretation. Instead, the spaces he creates enclose the viewer along with the figure; they cast the viewer in the role of voyeur, looking in on some obscure private ritual. The settings are painted with flat, brilliant colors against which the pieces of furniture and banal objects—a light bulb, a switch—are placed like the actual objects in a Cubist collage. To Bacon, these items are "certainties": they are easily recognized bits of familiar reality that, by their corroborative presence, make the horror of the contorted figures true to life.

The Picture and the Viewer

The way that the pictorial space draws the viewer in is accentuated in the triptychs, a format virtually reinvented by Bacon for modern art. Different from traditional triptychs, where the sequence of panels often tells a story, Bacon made of them an involving space extending around the viewer, forcing us into intimate contact with the figures, pushed toward us from their bare enclosures.

"Real imagination . . . is in the ways you think up to bring an event to life again. It is in the search for the technique to trap the object at a given moment." Thus Bacon sums up his pictorial strategy, which renounces any type of symbolism. His canvases signify no abstract ideas, generate neither icons nor emblems, only images for which interpretation, in the strict sense of the word, is inappropriate. We come upon them as if upon an accident. Their impact is overwhelming, like some obscene fragment of existence before which it is impossible to remain distant and aloof.

Francis Bacon/1909–1992

Although he was born in Dublin and spent most of his childhood in Ireland, Francis Bacon must be considered an English painter, for that was his family's origin. His father trained racehorses in Dublin until he entered the War Office and moved with his family to London at the outbreak of World War I. Until 1925 the Bacon family moved frequently between England and Ireland. The continual moves, along with the fact that he suffered from asthma, prevented the young Bacon from attending school regularly, and he received his education mostly from tutors.

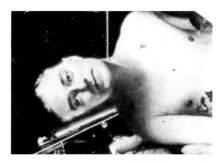

Photograph of wrestlers from Eadweard Muybridge, The Human Figure in Motion, *1887.*

Becoming an Artist

In 1925, Bacon left his family and settled in London. After a brief sojourn in Berlin, he spent two years in France, part of the time near Chantilly. There he frequently visited the Musée Condé and saw Nicolas Poussin's *Massacre of the Innocents* (1630–31). The figure of the mother crying out when her child is torn from her greatly impressed Bacon, to the point of becoming a recurrent image in his first paintings. So did another famous cry, that of the wounded nurse with shattered eyeglasses in the scene on the Odessa Steps from *Battleship Potemkin* (1925), the renowned film by Sergei Eisenstein.

Picasso's exhibition at the Paul Rosenberg gallery in Paris in 1927 decided Bacon on a career in painting. The work of the older artist revealed to him that within the human form was a new, unexplored world whose inner drama could be brought to the surface. This would become Bacon's pictorial world.

Medical photographs of a kind that inspired a number of Bacon's figure paintings; from K. C. Clark, Positioning in Radiography, *1929.*

Early Career

Settling definitively in London in 1928, Bacon soon earned a certain reputation as an interior decorator and furniture designer. Painting, which he began as a self-taught student, gradually gained more and more importance until it became his only activity. Little is known of his works from the 1930s, since Bacon himself destroyed most of them. In 1936 he submitted a picture to the "International Surrealist Exhibition," but it was rejected, perhaps a premonition that his work belonged not to the world of dreams and fantasies, but to the experience of the material world. In 1945 he established himself with the exhibition of *Three Studies for Figures at the Base of a Crucifixion* (plate 2), which explores the format of the triptych, and *Figure in a Landscape* (plate 11). He was associated at that time with other contemporary English figurative painters, like Graham Sutherland and Matthew Smith, as well as with the sculptor Henry Moore, and showed with them in several exhibitions. However, his incorrigible individuality was already apparent in canvases introducing his

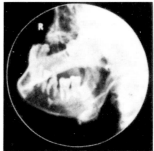

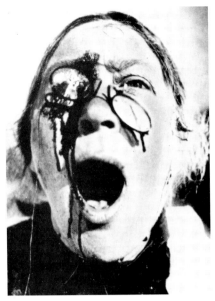

Still from Sergei Eisenstein's Battleship Potemkin, *1925, a source of the shrieking figures in Bacon's early paintings.*

characteristic concerns. The primal scream he discovered in the work of Nicolas Poussin and in the scene from Eisenstein gave rise to works such as *Head VI* (plate 1), *Study after Velázquez's Portrait of Pope Innocent X* (plate 3), and *Study for a Portrait* (plate 40). These were among the most outstanding compositions he had produced by the early 1950s.

Portraits and Figures

Bacon began to use X-ray photographs in his work to give a sense of flesh-and-blood realism to his portraits and figure paintings. As part of his quasi-scientific search for the reality of the body, he also made use of the photographic studies of figures and animals in motion realized by Eadweard Muybridge at the end of the nineteenth century. These sources became points of departure for many of Bacon's canvases. Another major concern was the relationship between the figure and the pictorial space, a relation that became more sharply defined; there appeared linear cubes that isolated the figures from their surroundings like transparent cages.

Bacon's international career was launched with his first solo show in New York in 1953 and his selection the following year, along with Ben Nicholson and Lucian Freud, for the Venice Biennale. In the 1960s, Bacon reached a new level of artistic achievement. Returning to the format of the triptych, he created *Three Studies for a Crucifixion* in 1962 (plate 5), transforming one of the central themes of his artistic career.

Additionally, the impact of his painting became more immediate, as can be seen in his portraits. Bacon painted persons from his circle of friends: their faces and names are now familiar to all devotees of the artist's painting, and they include Isabel Rawsthorne, Henrietta Moraes, Lucian Freud, and George Dyer. Bacon said that he never painted portraits of anyone except those close to him, since "if they were not my friends, I could not do such violence to them." Dyer was the most frequent model in the canvases of the 1960s, and his death in 1971 would weigh heavily on the artist.

The striking effect of Bacon's paintings and the carnal connotations of many of them extended his fame in this period beyond strictly artistic circles. The many exhibitions throughout the world devoted to Bacon's work consolidated his reputation, especially the retrospectives at the Tate Gallery, London, in 1962 (a second exhibition would be held there in 1985), and the Solomon R. Guggenheim Museum, New York, in 1963.

A Solitary Path

Francis Bacon was one of the most powerful figurative painters of this century. His achievement is all the more remarkable since he emerged from an artistic setting that was, during the 1940s and 1950s, dominated by abstract art. Though postwar British art produced a number of important creators—Graham Sutherland, Lucian Freud, R. B. Kitaj, David Hockney—the implacable independence of Bacon's work resists all academic classification. As with other great figurative painters of his time—the Frenchman Balthus, the Spaniard Antonio López, or Bacon's friend Lucian Freud—his was a solitary path, difficult for imitators to follow, but leading to a unique view of the spirit of the age. Francis Bacon remained active until the last year of his life. He died during a visit to Madrid in 1992.

Detail of Nicolas Poussin's Massacre of the Innocents, *1630–31, a painting that deeply affected Bacon.*

Plates

Myth and Tragedy

In the evolution of Francis Bacon's art, especially in its initial stages, several motifs are repeated frequently. Some of them come from specific paintings of the past, such as the portrait of Pope Innocent X by Velázquez, the Eisenheim Altarpiece by Matthias Grünewald, or the Crucifixion by Cimabue. Others come from myths recounted in literature, as with the themes taken from the Greek tragic poet Aeschylus or from T. S. Eliot. When Bacon uses such materials, it is not a question of retelling their stories or giving a literal re-creation of earlier pictures, but rather of stripping those original structures down to their essential human content. If Bacon used themes from those sources to surround his work with an aura of tragedy, he did so in order to suggest what evoked the primal scream shown in his early canvases—the intimate violence of real things. These recurrent motifs therefore function as meeting points between one's individual life experience and a larger sense of myth—that ancestral repository which has managed to preserve forms of representation appropriate to complex, difficult subjects throughout the ages. The Crucifixions, the bullfighting scenes, and the references to tragic literature selected by Bacon thus have in common an urge to deal with conflicting feelings and unknown forces—an urge, indeed, toward catharsis. Beyond the individual interest of each work, these canvases provide the key to the type of relationship Bacon sought to establish between viewers and his paintings, something similar to the attitude we might assume before a ritual whose meaning is unknown to us.

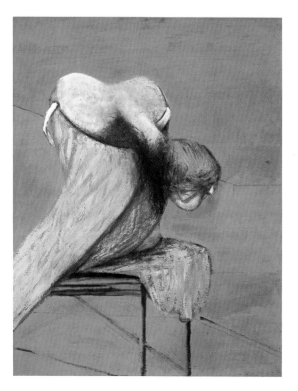
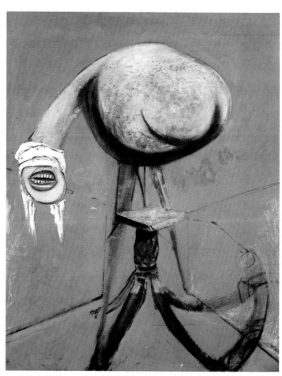

1 Head VI, *1949. The first trace in Bacon's work of the portrait of Pope Innocent X by Velázquez. The primal scream is the outstanding motif of these first canvases, where nearly the entire face disappears in shadow, leaving only the mouth that utters the cry. The background is a sort of curtain of shadows from which the figure emerges.*

2 Three Studies for Figures at the Base of a Crucifixion, *1944. The reference to the Crucifixion theme is only oblique—three figures, the idea of mutilated bodies. The bulbous forms bear a certain similarity to the monsters in some Surrealist canvases, a movement with which Bacon's work had some early affinity. More than four decades later, the artist painted a second version of this composition (plate 68).*

1

2

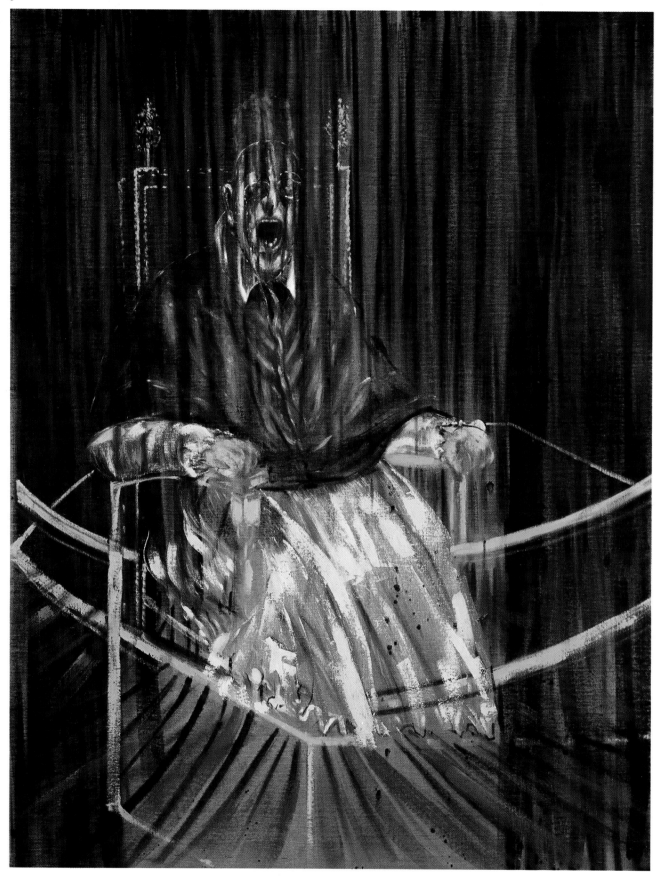

3 Study after Velázquez's Portrait of Pope Innocent X, *1953. The veil placed between the viewer and the figure of the Pope crying out derives from the textures of X-ray plates that Bacon often utilized in those years. The open mouth can be understood also as the result of a relaxing of the jaw that occurs in cadavers, which would well suit the spectral aspect of this figure.*

4 Study after Innocent X, *1962. A later version of the Velázquez theme where the cry no longer appears. The color has become lighter, and the spatial arrangement already characteristic of Bacon is present in all its elements: the transparent cage, the perspectival space that leaves the foreground empty, drawing the viewer in. Finally, the papal throne has been synthesized into simple volumes.*

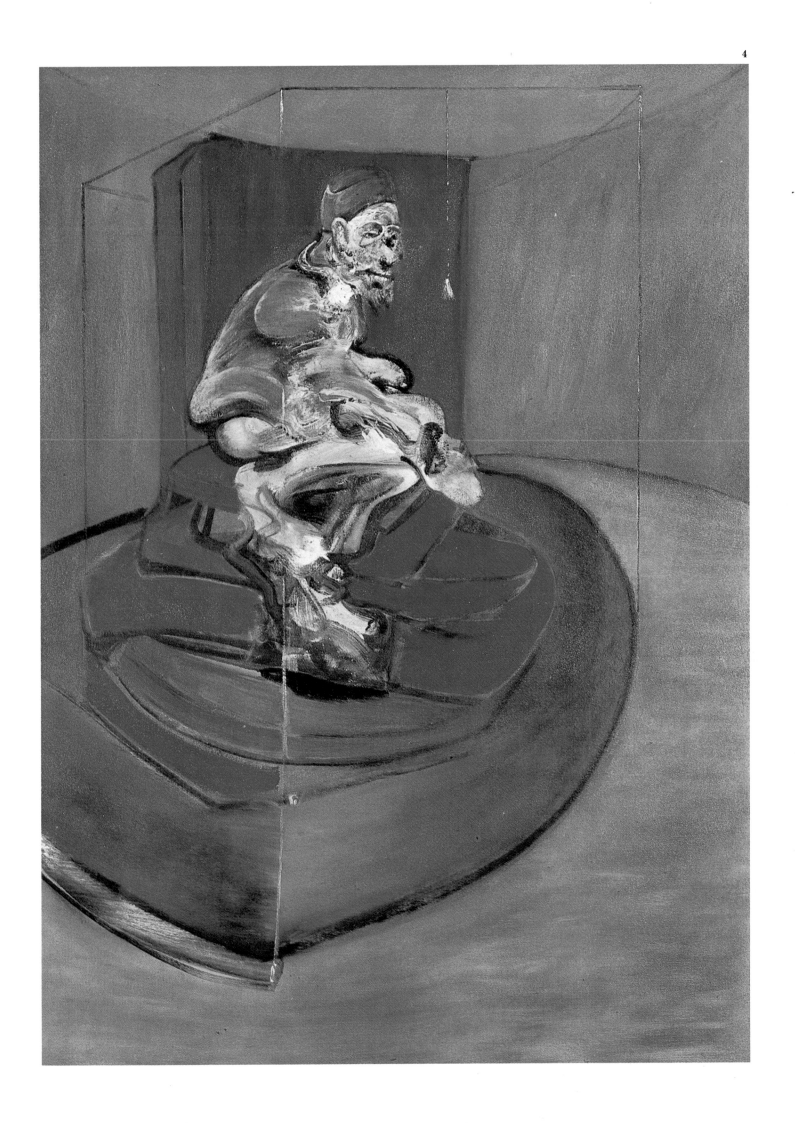

5 Three Studies for a Crucifixion, *1962. Almost twenty years after* Three Studies for Figures at the Base of a Crucifixion *(plate 2), Bacon returned to its evocation of sacramental slaughter and to its triadic structure. The panel to the right represents an animal's carcass slit open, but its form was suggested by a thirteenth-century Crucifixion by Cimabue, when seen upside down.*

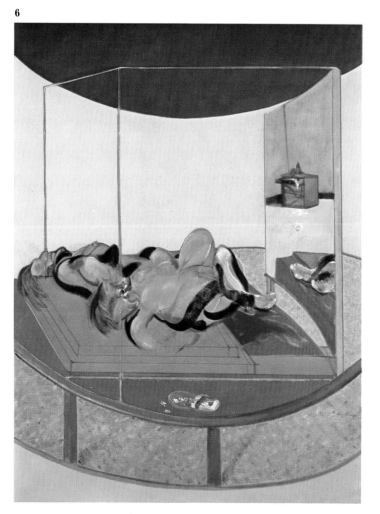

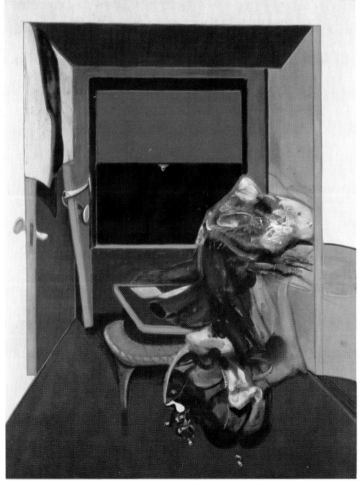

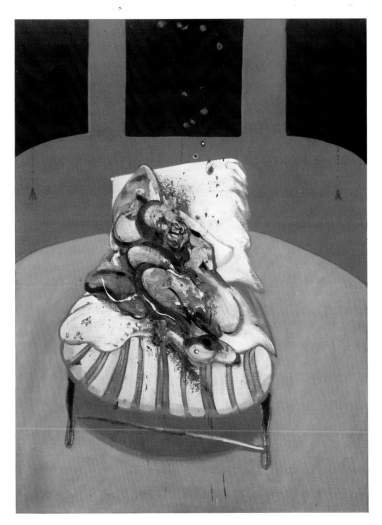

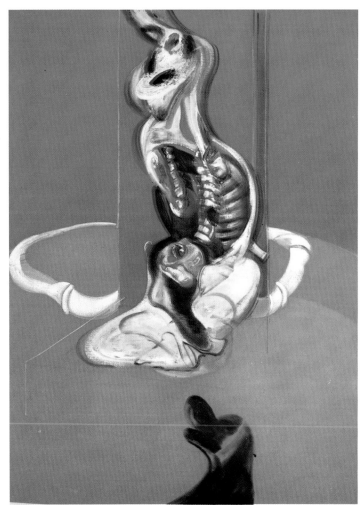

6 Triptych Inspired by T. S. Eliot's Poem "Sweeney Agonistes," *1967. Bacon refers to the line from Eliot's poem that summarizes life as "birth, and copulation, and death," the three acts—according to some interpreters—to which the three panels refer. The joined pairs on their platforms, right and left, derive from the photographs of naked wrestlers taken by Eadweard Muybridge.*

7

8

7, 8 Studies for Portrait of Van Gogh II and VI, *1957.* *Throughout the year 1957, Bacon completed several variations on the painting by Vincent van Gogh called* The Painter on the Road to Tarascon *(1888); they are rare attempts in Bacon's career to present an integrated treatment of figure and natural surroundings. Unlike his reminiscences of Velázquez, Rembrandt, or Muybridge, here the painter starts from something like the pictorial and chromatic character of the original.*

9, 10 Study for Bullfight No. 1, *1969;* Second Version of "Study for Bullfight No. 1," *1969. Bacon was interested in bullfighting as a tragic ceremony, comparable in a way to Aeschylus's* Oresteia *or the Crucifixion. It is himself that the painter depicts in the ring, becoming a single form with the bull at the consummation of their encounter. Their union is highlighted by the curved black brushstroke, above the full spread of the cape, that connects the two. The painting's luminous flat hues give a certain emotional distance to the spectacle.*

9

10

11

11 Figure in a Landscape, *1945. The image of the person seated on the park bench is fused with the surroundings, emerging from them in an unexpected fashion. Bacon had not yet developed the kind of pictorial space that appears in the 1950s.*

12 Study for a Crouching Nude, *1952. The tension in this figure derives directly from Michelangelo's nudes. Yet the figure is given an elusive, almost vaporous pictorial treatment that contrasts with the definite linear prism in which it is contained. It contrasts as well with the circular space, like a circus ring, whose rigid physicality is emphasized by the numerical calibrations marked on the railing behind the figure.*

Figure and Space

The concept of representation takes on a double meaning in Bacon's painting, for his works can be understood in almost theatrical terms. From the 1950s onward a clear difference can be observed between the treatment of the figure—violent, distorted, riven with complexities—and the treatment of the space around it, which is arranged like a bare stage. The contrast between the highly charged figure and its relatively neutral, flat surroundings is part of the visual theater designed by the artist; he places the painting's viewer in the same situation as a spectator at a peep show—confronting a figure displayed at a moment of profound intimacy, held in a linear box like a cage. It is made clear that the space enclosing the figure encompasses the viewer as well, since the box is simply an extension of the viewer's lines of perspective.

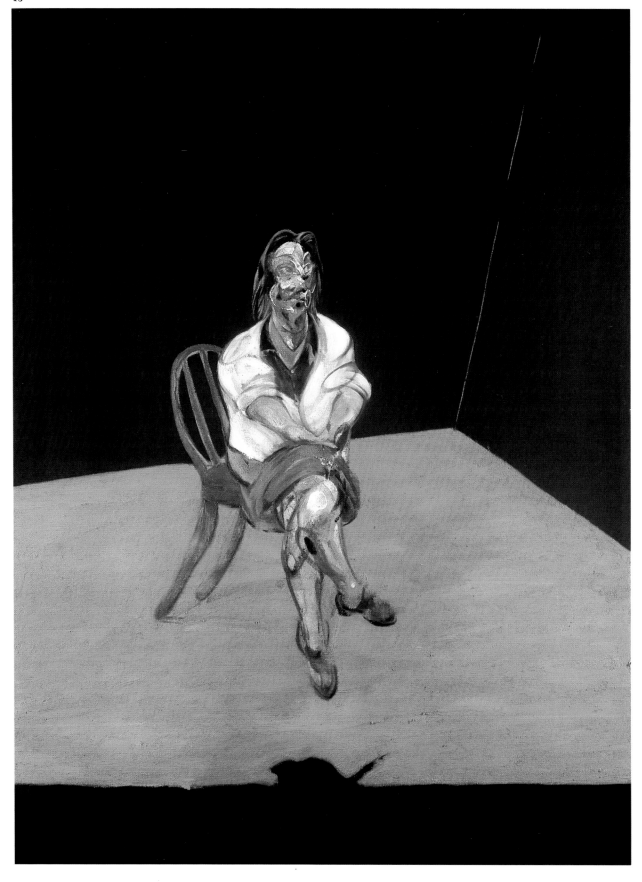

13 Study for a Portrait (Isabel Rawsthorne), *1964. The lack of spatial coordination between the subject and the chair on which she sits—a constant in many of the painter's portraits—reveals to what extent they obey different pictorial systems. The picture's effect arises from this contradiction.*

14 Portrait of Lucian Freud on a Sofa, *1965.*
The human figure focuses all the energy of the
canvas, absorbing everything around it. The
massive rotundity of the sofa seems to deflate
behind the figure, at the point of contact
between figure and setting.

15, 16 Lying Figure with Hypodermic Syringe,
1963; Lying Figure, *1969. The same subject*
is repeated with six years' difference. In
the second version the motif of the needle
disappears, and instead the light bulb and
switch appear, activating the space above
the figure.

15

16

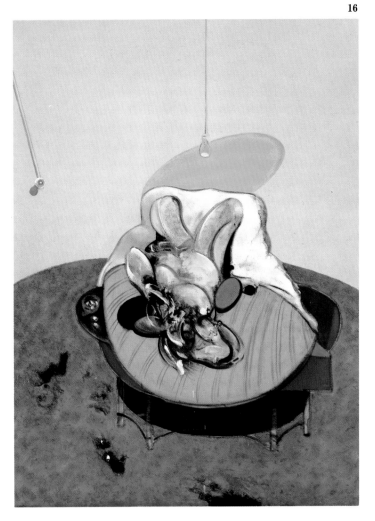

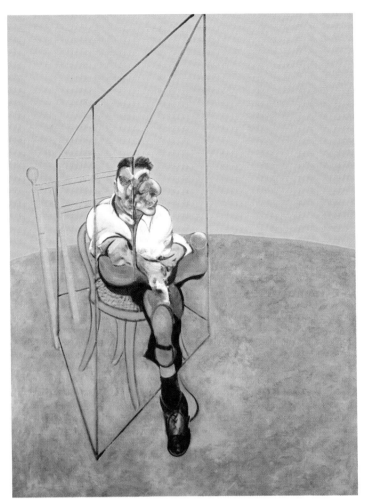

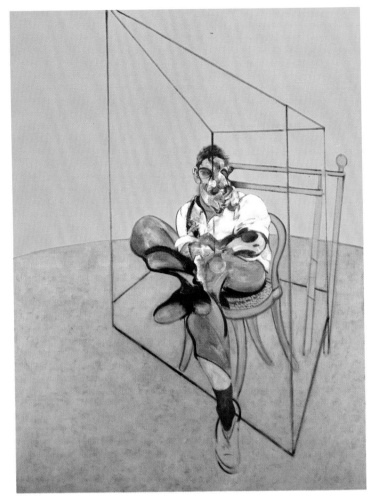

17

17 Three Studies of Lucian Freud, *1969. The triptych multiplies the visual possibilities in the interplay between figure and surroundings. The turning of the spatial prism encasing the figure in each panel generates a sequence of facial distortions. In the left panel, the different facets of the prism produce the faceted presentation of the face, shown in both frontal and profile view simultaneously, as Picasso had done.*

18 Three Studies of the Male Back, *1970. The different positions of the mirror offer a paradoxical sequence, whose aim is to disturb and question the relationship of the viewer to the painting. The high, diagonal point of view, as in an architect's axonometric drawing, accentuates the idea of the individual surprised in his privacy.*

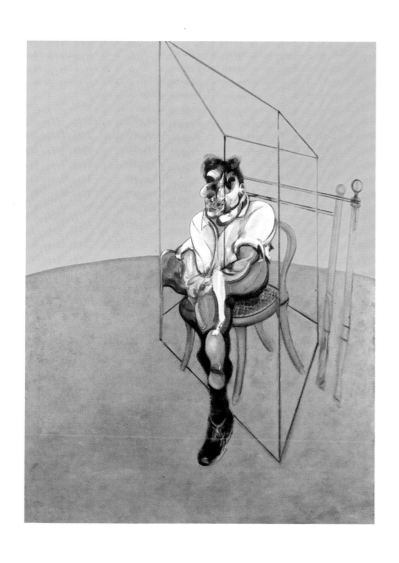

19 Portrait of George Dyer Talking, *1966. The light bulb and swinging tassel hanging from the ceiling accentuate the spiral space enveloping the figure. Bacon takes this idea from several Italian Renaissance painters, such as Piero della Francesca, who depicted an egg hanging on a string from the cupola that protects the figure in his famous Madonna in the Pinacoteca Brera in Milan.*

20

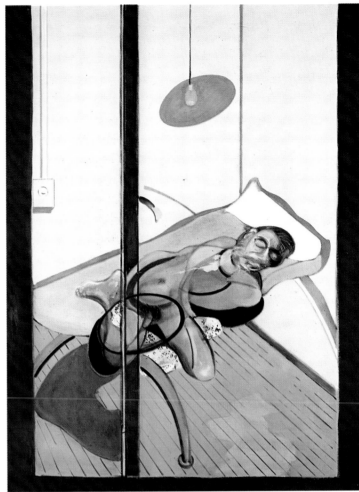

21

22

20, 21 Seated Figure, *1974; Sleeping Figure, 1974.*
Two examples of how the painter exploits the
relationship between figure and space. In these two
canvases the figure appears trapped in his pose,
crushed against the chair or the bed as though he
were only a vestige of himself, his mere lifeless skin,
molded by the pressing weight of the surrounding
space upon him.

22 Portrait of Isabel Rawsthorne Standing in a Street
in Soho, *1967. Bacon rarely places his figures in an*
exterior setting. When he does, the theatrical artifice
of his painting becomes more evident. In this
painting, the street is suggested by means of a kind
of backdrop behind the linear box. However, the scene
does not lose its immediacy from this, and perhaps
because of that tour de force the canvas always
remained one of Bacon's favorites.

23 Figure Writing Reflected in a Mirror, *1976. The figure and its reflection are fused, like Siamese twins. The mirror offers an image of the back of the figure that is physically impossible, given the angle of the mirror's placement as seen in the canvas. The illegible text of the newspaper on the floor reinforces the paradoxical effect of the work.*

24 Two Seated Figures, *1979. The two figures, with the look of businessmen in the waiting room of a station, occupy a closed, domestic space. The surprising verisimilitude of the chairs derives from Bacon's early experience as an interior designer.*

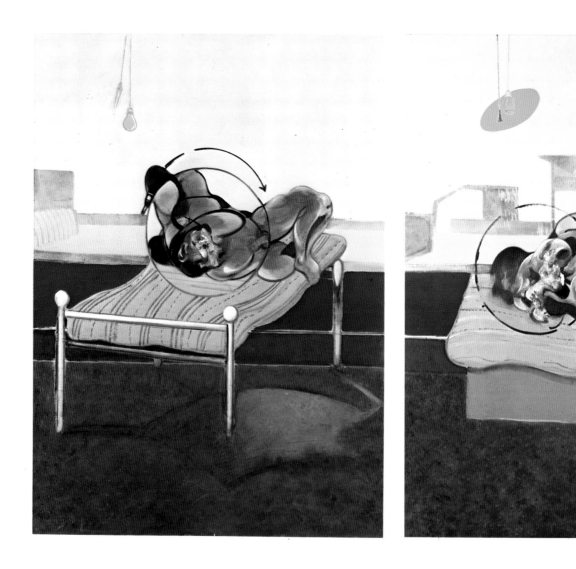

Violated Flesh

Bacon understood his figures as coming into being through a kind of creative violence; they were made manifest through his vigorous physical manipulation of the paint with his own hands. That material violence remains imprinted in what is depicted, in such a way that Bacon's figures appear as a turbulent mass of lacerated, wounded, tense flesh. In this respect even his paintings of the butchered carcasses of animals should not surprise the viewer; not only are they a natural outgrowth of his concern with the flesh-and-blood actuality of the body, but such depictions have a long history in art, as in some of the canvases of Rembrandt and other Dutch painters of the seventeenth century.

Equally important in Bacon's treatment of the body was the use of some photographs by Eadweard Muybridge that analyzed movement through sequential images of wrestlers (see page 6). Bacon transformed those detached, frozen scenes into violently carnal confrontations, exploiting all their potential for aggressive, orgiastic combat.

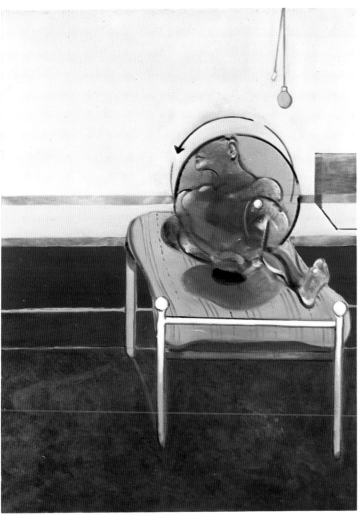

25

25 Three Studies of Figures on Beds, *1972. The figures struggling on the bed derive from Eadweard Muybridge's photographs of wrestlers (see page 6). Their contorted positions constitute the canvas's whole substance, to the point where it is almost impossible to distinguish one body from another: we see a single mass of flesh whose muscular torsion is reinforced, with the coldness of a diagram, by the circles and arrows superimposed by the painter.*

26 Blood on the Floor: Painting, *1986. Bacon always wanted his paintings to assume the material identity of what they depicted, in the most direct form possible. The drops of paint used to create the bloodstain, as though someone had actually bled on the canvas, are a good example of how Bacon sometimes initiated his images, and suggest how his concept of representation is to be understood.*

27, 28 Painting, *1946; Second Version of "Painting 1946," 1971. This macabre picture,
in which a terrifying figure with clerical garb sits in the midst of a scene of slaughter,
was one of the works that brought international recognition to Bacon, when it was
acquired by the Museum of Modern Art, New York, in 1948. The umbrella motif,
repeated in other works of this period, is the forerunner of the linear prisms that later
delimit the space around the figure. Twenty-five years later, Bacon returned to the
same theme, although the figure now wears a business suit and a raincoat, and the
artist's palette is brighter.*

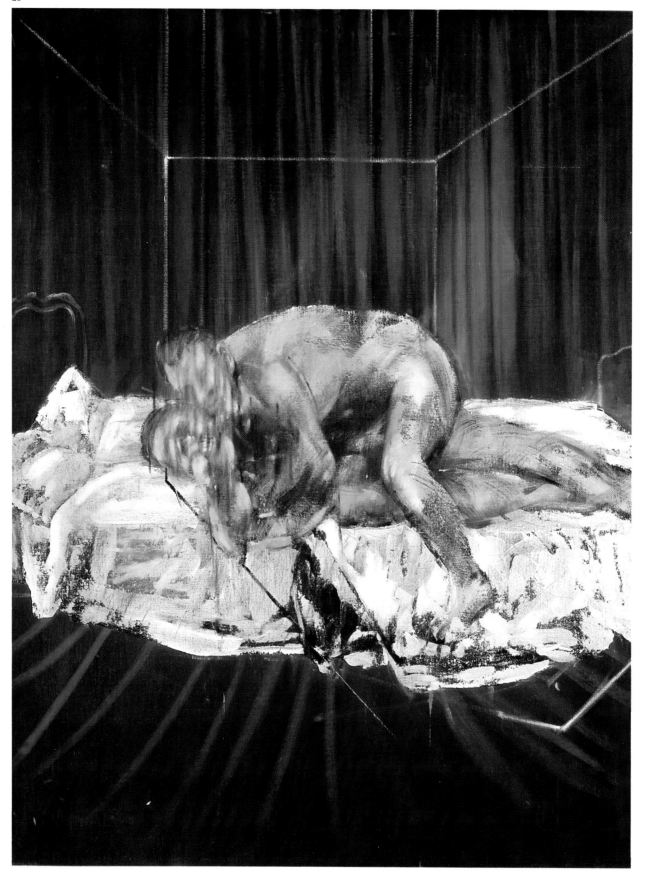

29 Two Figures, *1953. One of the first appearances of Muybridge's wrestlers (see page 6). By changing the figures' setting, Bacon has changed the athletic struggle of the original photograph into a passionate, even violent sexual encounter.*

30 Carcass and Bird of Prey, *1980. At a late date, Bacon again presents us with an image of butchered meat. And in a depiction based on the earlier use of X-ray pictures, the bird of prey is shown with a fleshless skull.*

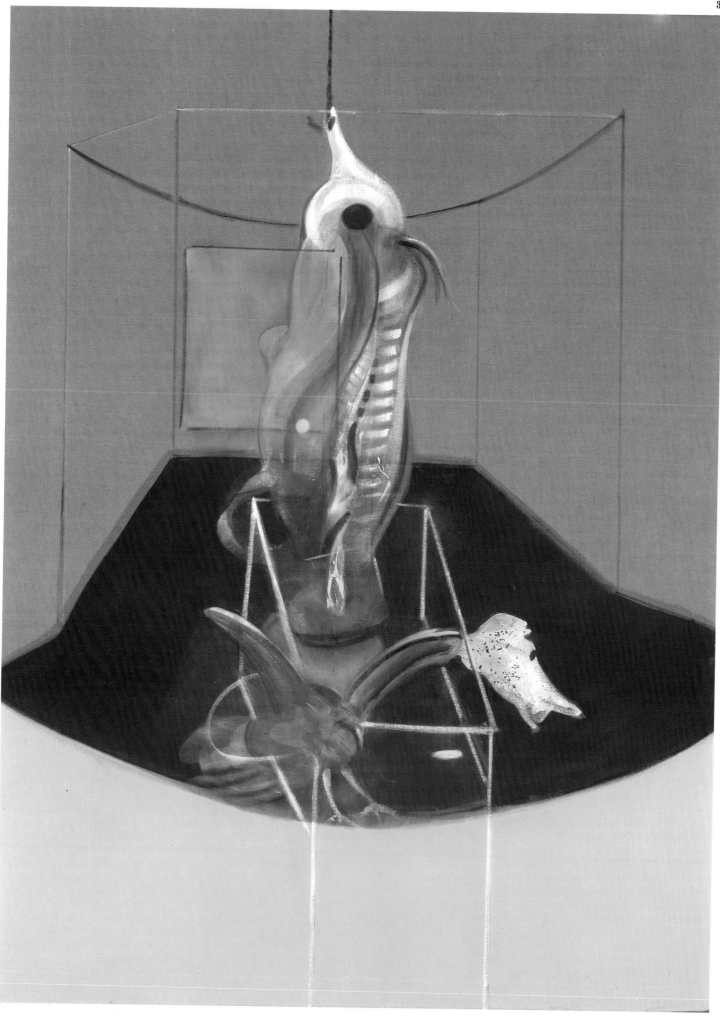

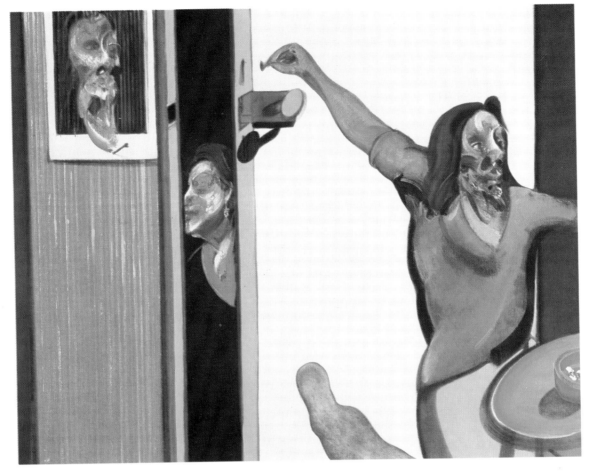

31   Three Studies
of Isabel
Rawsthorne, *1967.
The sequence of
images seen in the
triptychs is here
condensed into a
single panel,
with a separate
rectangular area
for each face. One
of the three studies
is presented as a
picture pinned to
the wall.*

Figure and Movement

"Michelangelo and Muybridge are mixed up in my mind together, and so I perhaps could learn about positions from Muybridge and learn about the ampleness, the grandeur of form from Michelangelo. . . . As most of my figures are taken from the male nude, I am sure that I have been influenced by the fact that Michelangelo made the most voluptuous male nudes in the plastic arts." Bacon here describes two of the sources from which his work derives. It is not so much the representation of movement itself in Muybridge that interests him as a certain sense of ritualized action that the poses convey. Similarly, it is not simply the imposing muscular tension of Michelangelo's nude figures—their famous *terribilità*— that affects him. In contrast, the tension within Bacon's figures, so often in awkward or unlikely positions, is nervous and tentative. What he seeks to create on the canvas is a sense of the figure as the center of swirling energies—in its movement or in its own inner tension. And he conveys those energies through the traces of the moving hand that wields the paintbrush.

32   Figure in Movement, *1976. The circles,
functioning like magnifying glasses on
the foci of tension, and the arrows that
complete the basic directions of movement
in an analytical fashion, are two sources
of dynamism in Bacon's canvases. The
fusion of two successive positions in
a single figure, like a stroboscopic
photograph, has been a feature employed
by painters since the time of the Futurists,
but it takes on a distinctive sense in Bacon.*

33 Portrait of George Dyer Riding a Bicycle, *1966. The figure exhibits many of its dynamic possibilities: the direction of the bicycle, the positions of the leg pedaling, and the face viewed both frontally and in profile. The resultant whirlwind frozen in motion lends intensity to a seemingly innocuous image.*

34 Figure in Movement, *1985. The cricket shin guards and the position of the arms reveal the origin of the figure. Its muscular tension is reinforced by the narrow door frame, a device learned from Michelangelo's sculptures and paintings.*

37

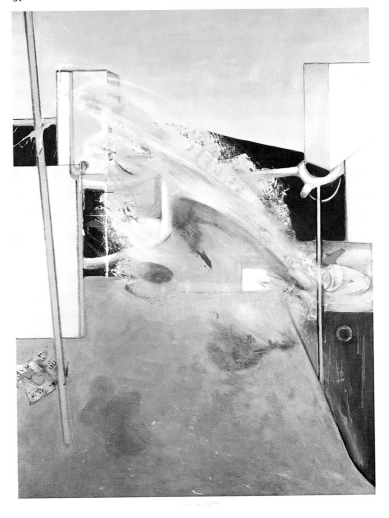

35 From Muybridge—Studies of the Human Body— Woman Emptying a Pail of Water and Paralytic Child on All Fours, *1965. Another transposition of Muybridge's photographs from which Bacon took physical movement to create pictorial tension.*

36 Figure in Movement, *1978. The movement itself here seems to mold the forms of the body, another source of dynamic tension in Bacon's artistic language.*

37 Jet of Water, *1979. Bacon made pictures of water currents and sand dunes whipped by the wind, seeking to reproduce their dynamic behavior materially, through the very application of paint. They constitute another attempt to re-create experience with immediacy.*

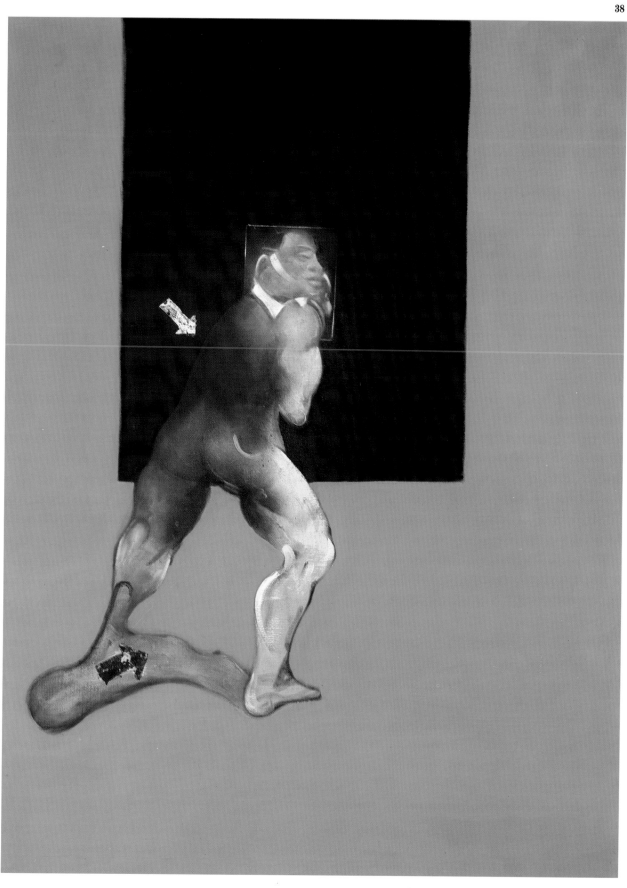

38 Study from the Human Body, *1987. Movement, understood as the figure's internal tension, is here revealed with the maximum economy of means: the arrows; the contrast between the black square and the red one; the powerful flexing of the right leg; and the left foot, which dissolves into paint dragged from the brush.*

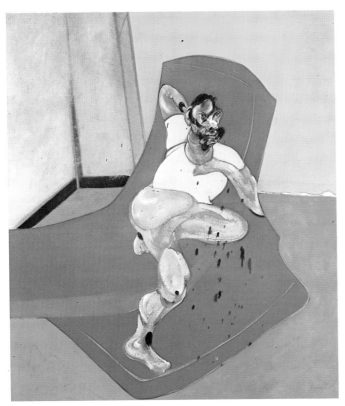

39

39 Double Portrait of Lucian Freud and Frank Auerbach, *1964.*
Bacon's friendships with the two figurative artists Frank Auerbach
and, in particular, Lucian Freud were not accidents. Even though
their work was quite different from Bacon's, they were among
the few contemporary artists whose pictorial universe one can
relate to Bacon's.

Portraits of Friends

The human presence is basic to all of Bacon's work. Thus it is not strange
that portraiture comprises the most abundant genre in his production. Yet
there is something unexpected about his painting portraits: in the pictorial tradition, the portrait has often been seen as a second-class form, and
its principal function, moreover, was illustrational. A portrait painter is
generally expected to illustrate the social or professional condition of the
subject. Bacon transformed what a portrait could be. In the 1960s his
closest friends became his models. In another unusual step, Bacon cus-
tomarily employed mundane snapshots as a reference rather than have
his models present. Painting from photographs helped Bacon maintain a
certain objective distance. Yet paradoxically, his freedom from the subjects' actual presence allowed him to re-create them with remarkable
immediacy. He said, "In trying to do a portrait, my ideal would really be
just to pick up a handful of paint and throw it at the canvas and hope that
the portrait was there."

40

41

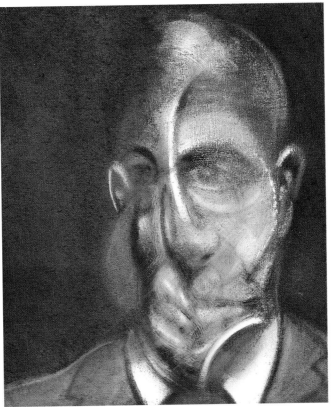

40 Study for a Portrait, *1953. The portraits made before the 1960s are somewhat generic, lacking particularized identities. They can be understood as the artist's reflections on the possibilities of the form, similar to the images based on Velázquez in the same period.*

41 Portrait of George Dyer in a Mirror, *1968. From the early 1960s until his death in 1971, George Dyer would be the portrait subject most frequently painted by Bacon.*

42 Portrait of Michel Leiris, *1976. A marked spatial break along one axis—generally the curve of the nose or the arch of the eyebrows—is one of the typical means employed in Bacon's portraits in order to disrupt the features of a face. This is no doubt a lesson he learned from the Picasso compositions of the twenties and thirties that Bacon had first seen in his youth.*

42

43 Three Studies for a Portrait (Peter Beard), *1975. Beard was the most frequent model for the portraits completed after the death of George Dyer. The circle superimposed on a part of the face is here also a means to distort its mass, as though part of the jaw or cheek were seen through a magnifying glass. These enlarged details probe the person's physical presence.*

44 Three Studies of Isabel Rawsthorne, *1966. The small portrait triptychs were inspired by police mug shots. What really interested Bacon, however, was the formulaic repetition of the head in different views— different attempts to capture the essence of the subject's face. Despite the deformation of the features, the face always remains recognizable, and is never reduced to a mask.*

45 Three Studies for a Portrait (Mick Jagger), *1982. The choice of a famous subject for this picture makes it possible to contrast the idea of the serial portrait as used by Bacon with its use by other artists, such as Andy Warhol, who also made multi-image portraits of the lead singer for the Rolling Stones.*

43

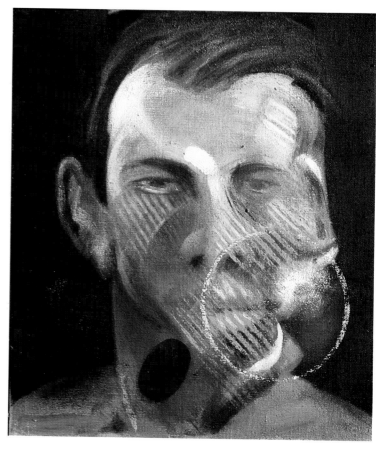

44

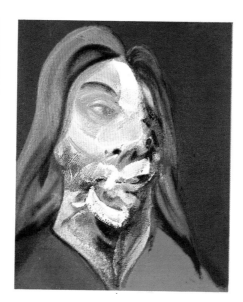
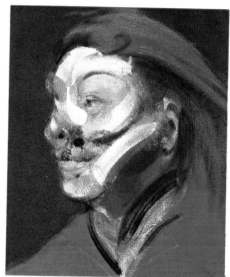

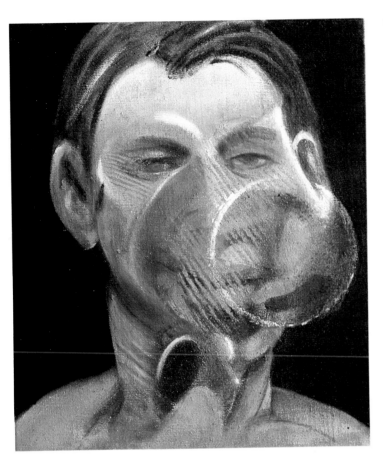
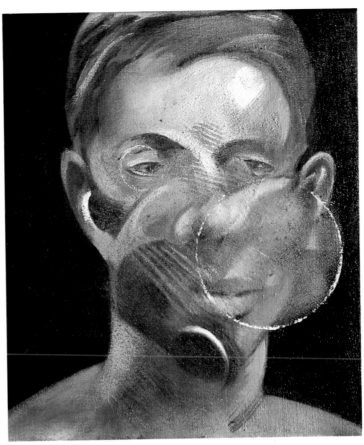

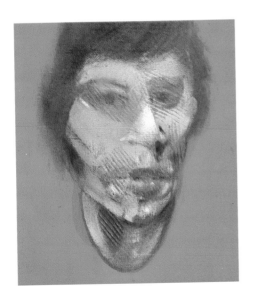
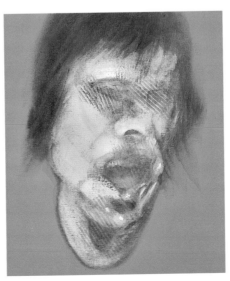
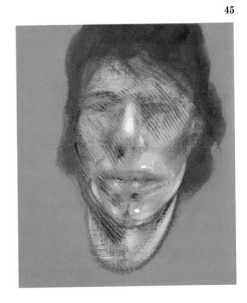

46

Self-Portraits

Although they are less renowned than his paintings of his intimate circle, Bacon frequently made portraits of himself. His series of self-portraits can be understood almost as a pictorial diary, but they show the same curious mixture of cold objectivity and intense immediacy as in his paintings of his friends. The method is, of course, the same as in the other portraits, dislocating the features by pulling them around the face's central axis. However great this distortion becomes, Bacon's subjects remain recognizable. Representation is pushed to that ambiguous moment when presence seems about to dissolve, but has not yet completely lost its distinguishing features.

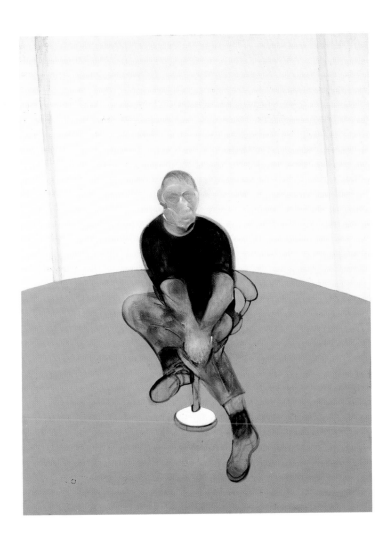

46 Study for a Self-Portrait, *1985–86.*
One of the last self-portraits made by
the artist, this image shows how
objective he could be. Bacon views
himself from an emotional distance,
without the vanity or narcissism
common in painters of all periods when
they choose themselves as a subject.

47 Self-Portrait, *1970. The painter*
depicts himself seated before a
completely blank canvas, giving his
personal twist to the portrait-of-the-
artist theme borrowed from the Old
Masters, who, in contrast, frequently
painted themselves at work, with palette
and brushes in hand. The raincoat,
reproduced with scrupulous exactitude,
plays the same naturalizing role as
the furniture and other domestic items
in Bacon's works.

47

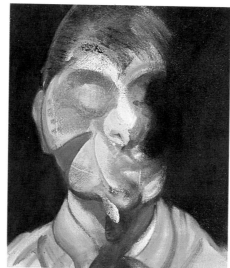
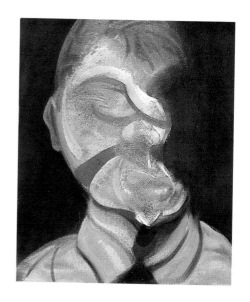

48

48 Three Studies for a Self-Portrait, *1972.*
*Three different aspects of the face are
shown, but without changing the position
of the head. Bacon employs only a few
brusque marks—the blue and white strokes
along the eye and nose, and the black zone
of the cheek—from which the viewer must
recompose the image. All the features are
concentrated in the right half of each face,
with the other half consumed by shadow.*

49 Self-Portrait with Injured Eye, *1972.*
*The inflamed eye serves as the basis for the
deformation of the entire face, taking
over one side completely and pushing the
remaining features to the other side.*

49

50, 51 Self-Portrait, *1972; Self-Portrait,*
1973. Two views of the painter in spatial
settings frequent in his works. In the first,
space is reduced to the series of planes
denoted by the differently colored
rectangles. In the second, the curved back
wall makes the space a cylinder, its floor
filled with the typical accessories of the
studio: the chair, table, light switch, and
the newspaper on the floor.

52

52 Self-Portrait, *1971. This is perhaps the most painterly of Bacon's self-portraits: the individual facial features are inseparable from the clearly evident brushstrokes that depict them. The light, too, is unusually pictorial: the countenance seems to emerge like a spectral presence from the penumbra of the background.*

53 Three Studies for a Self-Portrait, *1973. Bacon again concentrates the features on one side of the face, dislocating its symmetrical structure. The actual fingerprints on the picture surface reveal the artist's direct manipulation of the paint, as in a considerable number of his portraits. They constitute the visible evidence of Bacon's physical engagement with the pictorial material itself.*

53

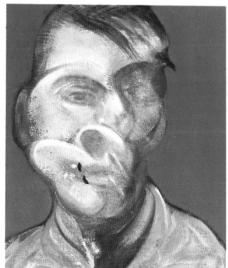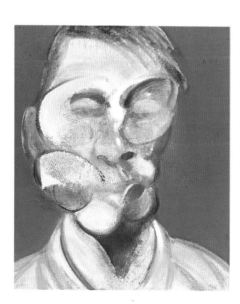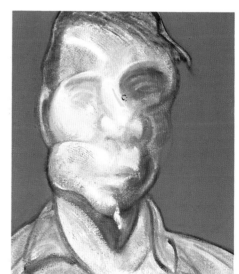

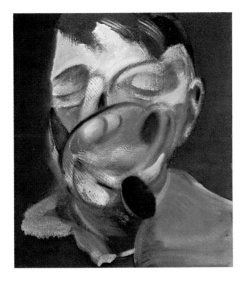  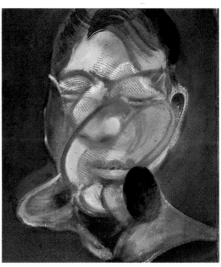

54

54 Three Studies for a Self-Portrait, *1974. A series of ovals joins one side of the face with the other. In each panel a somewhat different area of the face is emphasized by these means, although the view from panel to panel remains essentially frontal, as in the snapshots from automatic photo-booths that Bacon sometimes used (see page 6).*

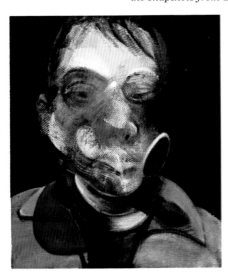 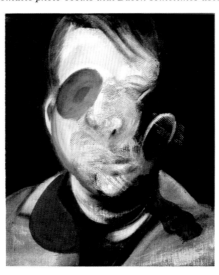 

55

55 Three Studies for a Self-Portrait, *1976. In these studies, Bacon plays with the possibilities of a cylinder, placed on a diagonal in each panel, which controls the organization of the picture.*

56

56 Three Studies for a Self-Portrait, *1979. Though the subject is always facing forward, a sequence from profile to front view to profile is created by changing the lighting from panel to panel and illuminating different areas of the face.*

Triptychs

The idea of a theater that parts the curtain on the figure in its most hidden intimacy culminates in the triptychs, the defining format in Bacon's painting. His sequences of images possess a sense not of narrative but rather of repetition. The fundamental objective is to involve the viewer in a suggestive setting, reinforcing the effect of the spatial boxes in which the figures are placed. In the preparatory studies for faces in portraits, Bacon used a smaller format clearly inspired by the frontal and profile photographs typical of police mug shots; he also made use of sequential snapshots taken by automatic photo-booths (see page 6).

57

57 Two Figures Lying on a Bed with Attendants, *1968. The three panels form one pictorial space and a single scene. The counterposed figures to the sides reinforce the doubling of the two figures on the bed.*

58 Two Studies for a Portrait of Richard Chopping, *1978. Although his most frequent choice was the triptych, Bacon's interest in the serial image occasionally produced double panels.*

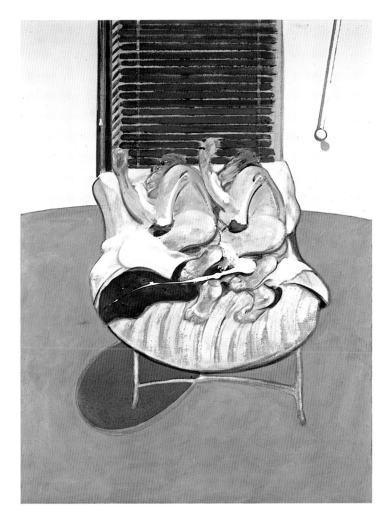

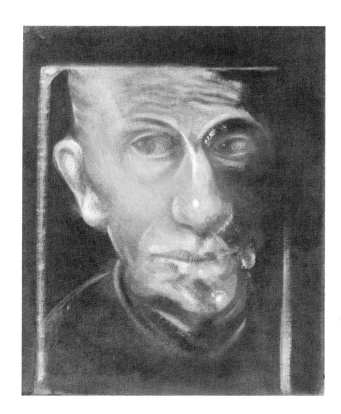

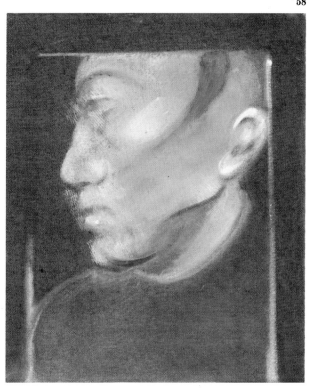

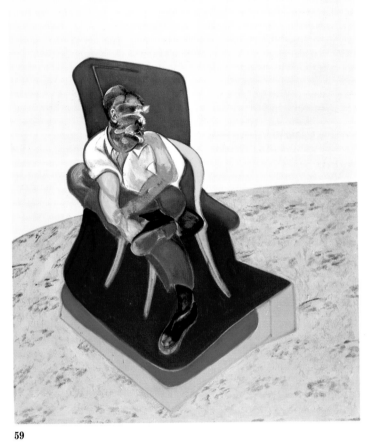

59

59 Three Studies for a Portrait of Lucian Freud, *1966. Bacon disturbs the symmetry typical of the triptych format by turning the figure in unexpected ways. Here, the frontal view of the face appears in the right-hand panel instead of in the central one, with the two profiles paired at the left.*

60 Studies of the Human Body, *1970. Muybridge's photographic studies reappear as a source of inspiration, producing images of the human body in positions awkward and tense to the point of becoming unrecognizable. The figure's precarious balancing act on the elevated bar increases the tension.*

60

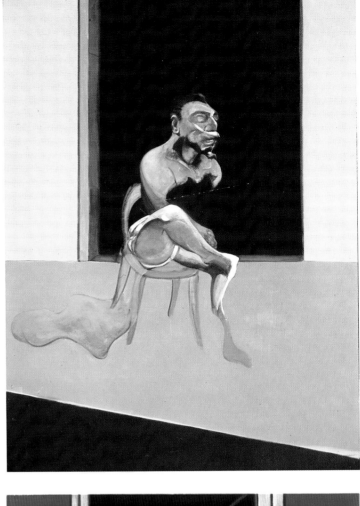

61 Triptych, August 1972, *1972. The three panels create a space subtly disturbed in its symmetry: there is a door in each panel, but of different size; and the scenes in the side panels are turned at slightly different angles with respect to the plane of the central canvas. The contrast between the bare, antiseptic setting and the mutilated figures produces an intensely dramatic effect with great sobriety of means.*

62 Triptych, May–June 1973, *1973. In this triptych the painter alludes to the circumstances of the suicide two years earlier of his friend George Dyer with horrifying precision. Yet the solemn harmony of purple and black lends the composition an unexpected ceremonial dignity.*

62

63

63 Three Portraits: Posthumous Portrait of George Dyer, Self-Portrait, and Portrait of Lucian Freud, *1973. The triptych format holds for Bacon a certain power of ritual evocation. This is seen in the encounter between his own image and those of two of his closest friends, one of them—George Dyer—already dead at that time.*

64 Triptych, March 1974, *1974. The figure in the central panel derives, once again, from Muybridge's photographs. The figures on the side panels open and close the composition: one, facing away, looks into the canvas, while the other—the photographer who seems to direct his camera lens toward the viewer— looks out from it. Both clothed figures contrast with the nude figure in the center panel and reinforce the immediacy of its presence.*

64

65 Triptych, *1976. These apparently arbitrary collections of images and diverse objects bear some resemblance to the dream logic of Surrealism, although they all in fact belong to Bacon's established repertoire: nude figures in tension, skeletal anatomies attacked by birds of prey, and so on. Everything seems to converge on the bloody ceremony depicted in the central panel, a ritual that the portrait busts on the side panels attend indifferently, like sphinxes—the guardians of a secret.*

66 Triptych, *1974–77. As in the composition shown above, there seem in this case to be certain points of contact with Surrealism, infrequent in Bacon's works. Also unusual is the suggestion of an open space, a beach perhaps. At the same time, the convoluted figures under their umbrellas or before a flat rectangle do indeed correspond to the mechanisms employed in other triptychs.*

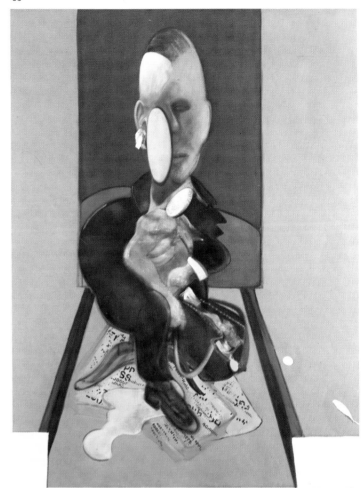

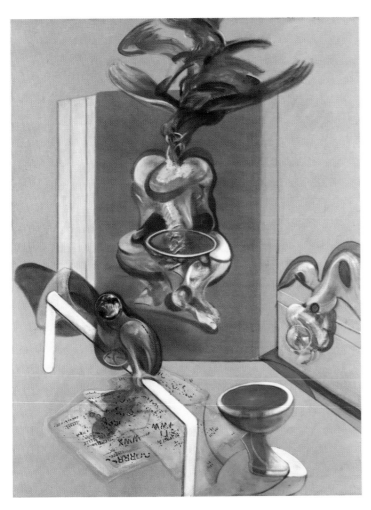

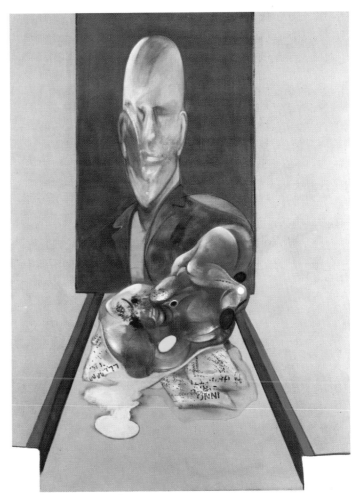

66

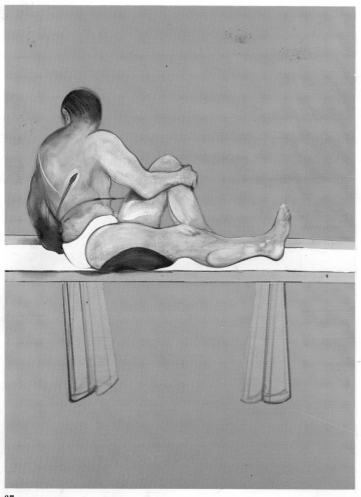

67

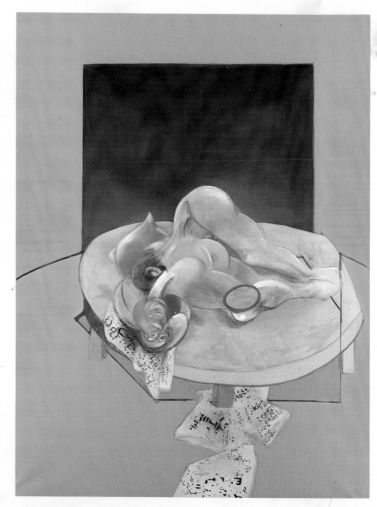

67 Triptych: Studies from the Human Body, *1979. The influences of Michelangelo and Muybridge, two of the presiding spirits in Bacon's works, are overtly combined in this canvas. The side figures are related to Michelangelo's funerary sculptures for the Medici Chapel in Florence. The central pair is, in turn, another version of Muybridge's wrestlers.*

68 Second Version of "Triptych 1944," *1988. Bacon here returns to one of his signature images, painting a second version of the Crucifixion that in 1944 had established the format of the triptych in his work (plate 2). The blind, bulbous figures are essentially the same, two having appendages that end in open mouths. What is different is the space in which they are placed, especially in the central panel, and the treatment of color, now darkly contrasting and more solemn, even elegiac.*

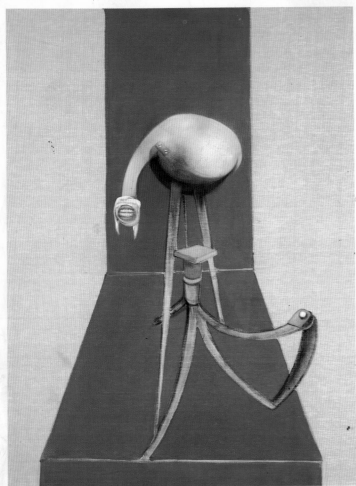

List of Plates

40 Study for a Portrait. *1953. Oil on canvas, 60 × 46½″ (153 × 118 cm). Kunsthalle, Hamburg*

41 Portrait of George Dyer in a Mirror. *1968. Oil on canvas, 6′6″ × 58″ (198 × 147.5 cm). Thyssen-Bornemisza Foundation, Madrid*

42 Portrait of Michel Leiris. *1976. Oil on canvas, 14 × 12″ (35.5 × 30.5 cm). Musée National d'Art Moderne, Centre Georges Pompidou, Paris. Gift of Michel and Louise Leiris*

43 Three Studies for a Portrait (Peter Beard). *1975. Oil on canvas; three panels, each 14 × 12″ (35.5 × 30.5 cm). Private collection, Madrid*

44 Three Studies of Isabel Rawsthorne. *1966. Oil on canvas; three panels, each 14 × 12″ (35.5 × 30.5 cm). Private collection*

45 Three Studies for a Portrait (Mick Jagger). *1982. Oil and pastel on canvas; three panels, each 14 × 12″ (35.5 × 30.5 cm). Private collection*

46 Study for a Self-Portrait. *1985–86. Oil on canvas; three panels, each 6′6″ × 58″ (198 × 147.5 cm). Marlborough International Fine Art*

47 Self-Portrait. *1970. Oil on canvas, 59.8 × 58″ (152 × 147.5 cm). Private collection*

48 Three Studies for a Self-Portrait. *1972. Oil on canvas; three panels, each 14 × 12″ (35.5 × 30.5 cm). Private collection*

49 Self-Portrait with Injured Eye. *1972. Oil on canvas, 14 × 12″ (35.5 × 30.5 cm). Private collection*

50 Self-Portrait. *1972. Oil on canvas, 6′6″ × 58″ (198 × 147.5 cm). Private collection*

51 Self-Portrait. *1973. Oil on canvas, 6′6″ × 58″ (198 × 147.5 cm). Private collection*

52 Self-Portrait. *1971. Oil on canvas, 14 × 12″ (35.5 × 30.5 cm). Musée National d'Art Moderne, Centre Georges Pompidou, Paris. Gift of Michel and Louise Leiris*

53 Three Studies for a Self-Portrait. *1973. Oil on canvas; three panels, each 14 × 12″ (35.5 × 30.5 cm). Private collection*

54 Three Studies for a Self-Portrait. *1974. Oil on canvas; three panels, each 14 × 12″ (35.5 × 30.5 cm). Collection Carlos Haume, Bogotá*

55 Three Studies for a Self-Portrait. *1976. Oil on canvas; three panels, each 14 × 12″ (35.5 × 30.5 cm). Private collection, Geneva*

56 Three Studies for a Self-Portrait. *1979. Oil on canvas; three panels, each 14.8 × 12.5″ (37.5 × 31.8 cm). The Jacques and Natasha Gelman Collection*

57 Two Figures Lying on a Bed with Attendants. *1968. Oil on canvas; three panels, each 6′6″ × 58″ (198 × 147.5 cm). Whereabouts unknown*

58 Two Studies for a Portrait of Richard Chopping. *1978. Oil on canvas; two panels, each 14 × 12″ (35.5 × 30.5 cm). Private collection*

59 Three Studies for a Portrait of Lucian Freud. *1966. Oil on canvas; three panels, each 6′6″ × 58″ (198 × 147.5 cm). Private collection*

60 Studies of the Human Body. *1970. Oil on canvas; three panels, each 6′6″ × 58″ (198 × 147.5 cm). Marlborough International Fine Art*

61 Triptych, August 1972. *1972. Oil on canvas; three panels, each 6′6″ × 58″ (198 × 147.5 cm). Tate Gallery, London*

62 Triptych, May–June 1973. *1973. Oil on canvas; three panels, each 6′6″ × 58″ (198 × 147.5 cm). Private collection*

63 Three Portraits: Posthumous Portrait of George Dyer, Self-Portrait, and Portrait of Lucian Freud. *1973. Oil on canvas; three panels, each 6′6″ × 58″ (198 × 147.5 cm). Galerie Beyeler, Basel*

64 Triptych, March 1974. *1974. Oil on canvas; three panels, each 6′6″ × 58″ (198 × 147.5 cm). Private collection, Madrid*

65 Triptych. *1976. Oil and pastel on canvas; three panels, each 6′6″ × 58″ (198 × 147.5 cm). Private collection, France*

66 Triptych. *1974–77. Oil and pastel on canvas; three panels, each 6′6″ × 58″ (198 × 147.5 cm). Marlborough International Fine Art*

67 Triptych: Studies from the Human Body. *1979. Oil on canvas; three panels, each 6′6″ × 58″ (198 × 147.5 cm). Private collection*

68 Second Version of "Triptych 1944." *1988. Oil on canvas; three panels, each 6′6″ × 58″ (198 × 147.5 cm). Tate Gallery, London*